Tactics of Success: Cricket

Cover illustration: Steve Waugh of Australia defends against England. His front pad is thrust forward and his bat held clear of the ball but his gloves are in the danger area for the ball that turns. Should the ball clip the gloves or bat as well as the pad then David Gower is close in to take the catch. (Colorsport)

Tactics of Success

Cricket

Michéle Savidge
Foreword by Geoff Arnold
Former England International and Coach, Surrey CCC

WARD LOCK

◀ A young Gary Sobers, pictured in 1957 forcing Fred Trueman into the off side from the back foot. The greatest all-rounder of his age – and perhaps any other – Sobers could bat defensively or with awesome attack, bowl as quick as most or with deft and accurate spin, and field anywhere, especially in the slips where a dropped catch was almost unheard of. (Colorsport)

© Ward Lock, 1992

First published in Great Britain in 1992
by
Ward Lock
An Imprint of Cassell
Villiers House, 41/47 Strand,
London WC2N 5JE

British Library Cataloguing-in-Publication Data:
a catalogue record for this book is available from the British Library

ISBN 0-7063-7088-0

Illustrations by Cilla Eurich.

Designed and edited by DAG Publications Ltd.
Designed by David Gibbons; typeset by Typesetters (Birmingham) Ltd, Warley, West Midlands; printed and bound in Great Britain by Clays Ltd, Bungay, Suffolk.

Contents

Foreword

By Geoff Arnold,
former England International and now County Coach/Cricket
Executive for Surrey C.C.C.

Cricket is not only a technical game but a tactical one too; the
team or individual which is more tactically aware will come out
on top. Furthermore, even if you are only a spectator you will
gain more enjoyment from watching the game if you come to
appreciate and recognise the strategies employed at the highest
level.

In this book you will find not only the skills and attributes
players must acquire to further their cricket expertise, your
memory will also be jogged by the author's examples of the techniques being used by international stars in major competitions. If
you look to improve your game by learning from your superiors –
there is no better way – then watch how they add to their
performance by the tactical use of skill and technique.

Whether you are a bowler, batsmen or fielder; whether
you are the star of your team or there to make the numbers up;
whether you are eight or eighty and even if your ambition is no
more than to be a more informed watcher of the game, your love
of cricket and your respect for its delightful complexity can only
grow by increasing your understanding of the *tactics of success*.

Introduction

Cricket is perhaps the most complicated sport to learn – and surely the most difficult to master. Even the most experienced cricketers admit they never stop learning, that there is always a new tactic or technique to be mastered.

This book is aimed at players at any level who are looking to improve their game, but it cannot claim to be a definitive guide because the game itself has so many variants. I do seek, however, to offer players a different view and make them more analytical in their approach to the sport.

Tactics can win or lose a game. Pre-planning is essential for coaches, captains and players if they are to make the most of opportunities. Adaptability must be a priority as well, though, for the unexpected is a frequent visitor to the cricket pitch and flexible tactical awareness should be the watchword.

This book is about winning – and how you can maximise your chances of success by your choice of tactics. I have assumed that readers are proficient in the basics of the game and that its terms are understood.

The examples of tactics are chosen for their tuitional value; I have tried not to be biased in favour of any particular player, team or country. It is not a coincidence, however, that West Indies cricket is extensively used, for it is that team which, at its best, has been proven in every discipline of the game and, furthermore, has been the fittest side in the business. A fit body and an alert brain have taken many a West Indian to the top of his profession, and recently the England team, under Graham Gooch, has sought to adopt the same philosophy.

A final word to those readers who might be surprised, if not alarmed, that a woman has written such a book. I have watched cricket for some twenty years, written about it for ten and cannot think of a match that I haven't enjoyed or learnt something from! And that is the beauty of cricket: there is a *tactic of success* to be learnt from every game.

▶ The apparent casual air shown by Viv Richards when batting demonstrates not only great confidence but also fine balance and extreme concentration. When moving from his crease to drive, his footwork is precise and well practised so as to get him to the pitch of the ball with the same readiness as he would have for a back foot defensive shot. (Colorsport)

Batting Conditions – Assessing the Pitch

Adjusting to the nature of the playing surface and prevailing atmospheric conditions can have a crucial bearing on the outcome of the game, particularly in limited-overs matches.

When the playing surface is dry at the beginning of a match, the team which bats first can usually enjoy the best batting conditions as the pitch can be expected to worsen through wear and tear, and any rain, as the game progresses. Their spin bowlers especially may also benefit from bowling second on a worn track.

How a particular pitch plays can also be affected by the amount of grass on it; pace bowlers will expect more seam movement from a well-grassed wicket.

As well as looking at the wicket, the batsman needs to assess the state of the outfield for he will be at a disadvantage if it is damp, and therefore slow. Such an outfield is not the same as one in the early morning where overnight dew will soon disappear. If the batsman feels at a disadvantage because of a slow, wet outfield, he can take comfort in remembering that slippery conditions can hamper bowlers and fielders too.

The current state of the weather is also a guide to assessing batting conditions for if the sky is overcast and the atmosphere humid this is likely to benefit bowlers seeking to swing the ball.

● Learning the Tactic

① Batsmen should endeavour to practise in all weather conditions and ask for various types of bowling so as to increase their experience.

② The ability to assess pitch conditions comes from experience, and older players should help younger team-mates refine the skill.

● The Tactic in Use

① If the outfield is slow and wet, the batsman must be prepared to make up the consequent loss of boundaries by his running between the wicket.

② If the conditions are conducive to swing, the batsman should be ready to encounter it. Forewarned is forearmed.

● Batting Conditions – Assessing the Pitch: Gary Sobers, West Indies v. England, Jamaica 1968

A thunderstorm has left the pitch wet. Colin Cowdrey, the England captain, decides to bat and England score 376. The West Indies are bowled out for 143 in 48 overs and Cowdrey enforces the follow-on. In the first innings, Sobers has been out LBW first ball to a shooter and in the second innings he comes to the crease at 174 for 4.

The first ball he faces from David Brown flies from a crack in the pitch to lob from the bat over Titmus' head at short leg. Two awkward cutters then find the edge, one falling in front of Graveney and the second being dropped by Basil D'Oliveira. Sobers has so far made seven.

Crowd trouble now delays the game for 90 minutes but when play resumes the pitch is still suspect – England keeper, Jim Parks, concedes 33 byes as the ball continually leaps over his head. But Sobers is hardly missing a delivery. Through supreme concentration he reaches his 50 in two hours and moves through the nineties taking singles, with the second 50 taking almost four hours. His innings of 113 not out is labelled a 'masterpiece of defence' from an aggressive batsman who, even in this innings, still managed to hit Titmus for 16 in one over!

Early shots must be cautious, correct and controlled.

The First Few Balls

● The Tactic

After assessing batting conditions and adjusting to them, the first few balls which the batsman faces can set the seal on the type of innings he is to play. It is the time at which batsmen will feel most nervous, even though some top class batsmen do not seem to play their first few balls so differently to those they face later – a combination of quality and experience.

The new batsman will be closely watched by the opposition skipper and his bowlers for tell-tale signs of strengths and weaknesses.

The situation of the game (see Tactic 3) can also dictate the manner in which the batsman plays the first few balls but, whatever the state of the game, he must do all he can to 'get his eye in' as quickly as possible.

● Learning the Tactic

① A batsman must train to get the basics of batmanship well set in his mind – his grip, stance, backlift, etc. – so that these factors do not affect his concentration early in his innings.

② Mental preparation is as vital as physical work. A batsman should be entirely aware of his specific role as he walks to the wicket and have absorbed as much information about the state of the game as possible.

● The Tactic in Use

① A batsman should never allow others to force him to hurry his preparation for the first ball.

② Though the batsman will be rightly eager to assert his authority from the first ball, he must bear in mind he loses all if he gets out quickly in an effort to exert that influence too soon.

③ However long the bowler's run-up, or however unusual, the batsman must concentrate on the bowler from the moment he begins his run until he releases the ball.

● The First Few Balls: Viv Richards, West Indies v. England, Antigua 1986

England have arrived in Antigua four down in the series after having lost all five tests at home in 1984.

Richards is determined to play a memorable innings in his home town of St Johns but has scored only 26 in the first innings before falling to Ian Botham.

West Indies have a lead on first innings of 164 and Richie Richardson and Desmond Haynes open with a further 100 before Richardson falls to Emburey. When Richards walks out the tea interval is only 28 minutes away but, after defending his first two balls, he takes three off his third before blasting Ellison and Emburey over midwicket for sixes. Gower spreads his field but Richards simply adjusts his shots.

Richards makes 28 runs off the 15 balls he faces before tea – an ominous indication of what was to come. He goes on to score 100 in 56 balls – the fastest century in Test cricket – with the second fifty coming off 21 balls against bowlers who were trying to contain him. He finishes his onslaught unbeaten on 110 after hitting Emburey for a huge six and declaring!

No respecter of reputations, Viv Richards could attack the first delivery he received.

The Game Situation

● The Tactic

The situation of the game will dictate how a batsman should play his innings. If, for example, his team is 27 for six, it is absolutely no use to his team-mates if he dances down the wicket to a good ball and is promptly stumped or bowled. Similarly, if his team has lost a wicket just before an interval, it is important that he play out the remaining balls before the break.

If, however, the batsman comes to the crease with his team needing 12 runs off the last six balls with one wicket remaining, he should be looking for *any* opportunity to score, even a single.

We have all seen experienced players choose the wrong course of action in pressure situations and the player who regularly fails to assess the game situation is either foolish or selfish, and of little value to any team.

● Learning the Tactic

① Though batting is very much an individual task it is played within a team game and new batsmen must listen to those who have batted, and especially to the colleague they join at the wicket, so that concensus on the game situation is achieved.

② In situations requiring defence the natural urge for quick running or adventurous shots must be curbed and, conversely, in a run chase players must try to 'change their spots' in the team's cause.

● The Tactic in Use

① The new batsman must have clear instructions from his captain and be the carrier of new tactical advice to the not out player.

② Understanding and good communication between the batting pair is never more crucial than in dire situations of defence or all-out attack. Batsmen who call clearly, act on each other's calls and take runs quickly and safely will prosper.

③ A batting pair in such situations may choose to try to face the bowler which most suits their abilities. Undertaken wisely and with caution, this can be a useful tactic.

● The Game Situation: Essex v. Nottinghamshire, Benson & Hedges Cup Final, Lord's 1989

This match generates a finish improbable even by the extraordinary standards set by one-day matches.

Essex, the favourites, seem to have the match well under control. Virtually the only moment, in fact, that Notts appear to have a remote chance of winning is when Eddie Hemmings faces John Lever, needing four runs off the last ball to take the trophy.

And that does seem a remote chance because 40-year-old Lever is a skilled hand at these situations while Hemmings, who is four days older than Lever, is less sprightly between the wickets than he has been.

Nine runs are needed at the start of the last over and Graham Gooch, the Essex captain,

and Lever now take three minutes to set a field to prevent the match-winning boundary being scored. They concentrate on the leg-side field but Hemmings makes room for himself and slices the straight, full-length ball on the offside. Hardie chases the ball with all his might but it beats him to the rope in front of the Grandstand and Nottingham-shire win by three wickets to take their first B&H Trophy.

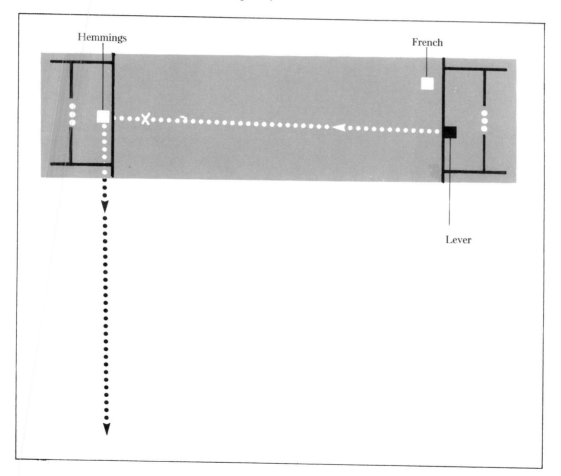

Awareness of Field Settings

● *The Tactic*

In top-class cricket, players are coached to be aware of the fielding limitations, and the likely choice of field placings, of their opposition. In club and youth cricket this is not so easy but a great deal can be quickly learned by an astute batsman during the course of a match.

The field positions set by an opposition captain can betray a weakness in his bowlers, but it can also demonstrate he has learnt how to counter a batsman's favourite stroke. Needless to say, a batsman must have a good basic knowledge of field settings, practise playing his shots to the inevitable gaps which are left and learn to exploit his opponents failures to set suitable fields.

● *Learning the Tactic*

① It is useful to use some net sessions to practise keeping the ball out of the hands of close fielders; attempt to play every ball into the ground short of the net, and have the bowlers try to prevent you doing so.

② Always take time to check the field which is being set for you and pay attention to those fielders who have strengths and weaknesses.

● *The Tactic in Use*

① The batsman should always be alert to positional changes in the field and, if he is distracted by such a move, he should pull back from his stance to make a full check.

② Not all batsmen have the aptitude to assess field placings so team-mates should always be ready to offer advice.

③ If the opposition has a particularly fast and adept fielder then take no risks to him, play the ball clear of him if you can, and thus both neutralise and frustrate him by taking him out of the game.

④ By definition, a fielder close to the wicket leaves a gap behind him; exploit this when you can.

● *Awareness of Field Settings: Derek Randall, England v. Australia, The Centenary Test, Melbourne, 1977*

In his first Test against Australia, Randall makes a remarkable 174 off some of the fiercest bowling Australia has ever produced. Dennis Lillee is at his intimidating best and the acrobatic Randall performs a full somersault at one stage whilst evading a Lillee bouncer.

Randall's colleagues have found it almost impossible to play the Aussie paceman in front of the wicket, with the result that the familiar 'umbrella' field is a common feature throughout the English innings. To counter this, the Nottinghamshire player sets out to play the fast bowlers through the poorly-marshalled covers area at every opportunity, contriving to irritate the bowlers to a point where they lose their accuracy to him. Lillee even tries bowling off a short run but this only sees Randall hit him for 10 runs in one over.

The innings is one of the finest examples of awareness of the fielding positions and of shot placement to evade them. Dennis Amiss calls the performance, 'One of the greatest of all time.'

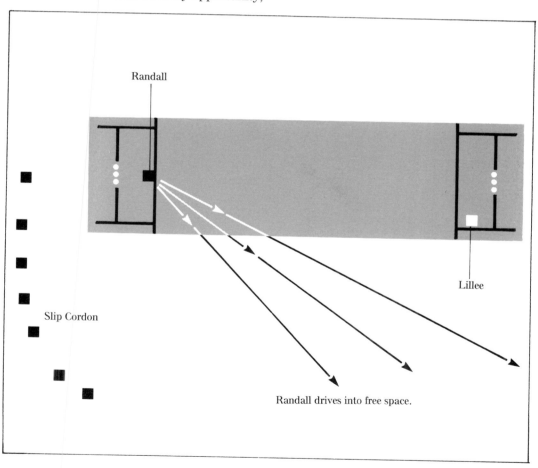

Randall

Lillee

Slip Cordon

Randall drives into free space.

◀ Joel Garner, the 6′8″ West Indian, captured in his delivery stride. Leading arm high, the seam of the ball pointing down the wicket and that huge front foot above bail height and about to thump into the crease to maximise the pace of the delivery. With the ball leaving his hand some nine feet from the ground, Garner's height was often too great for county sightscreens! (Colorsport)

▲ Alan Knott demonstrated all the physical attributes and tactical awareness of a great wicket keeper. Superbly agile, standing up to the wicket or further back, he was ever alert and would often act as a twelfth fielder by covering shots close to the wicket when the field was set deep. (Colorsport)

The Quick Single

● The Tactic

The ability to take the quick single is of great importance to any batsman, particularly in limited-overs matches when the run-rate has to be maintained. Even quality professional players can find themselves discarded for such games because of their lethargy between the wickets.

Fitness and quick reactions are the key to good running and adding singles to your score, where others might fail to do so, can win any type of match.

Both the bowler and his fielding team-mates can become irritated when perfectly accurate deliveries are defended *and still scored from*. The bowler may bowl more erratically as a result and the fielders can be induced to adjust their position to your benefit or panic in some other way.

The risk of taking a quick single is reduced as the understanding between the batsmen at the crease is improved.

● Learning the Tactic

① First get fit! Sprinting practice never harmed any batsman.

② Remember the basic rules: if he plays the ball in front of the wicket, the striker calls; if his shot runs behind the wicket, the non-striker makes the decision.

③ By sensible backing-up the non-striker can reduce his running distance to 15 yards.

④ The non-striker should bear in mind the difficulty his partner will have if asked to take a quick single when he has just played off the back foot.

● The Tactic in Use

① That batting is *two* men at work is never better demonstrated than in the team-work required for the efficient taking of quick singles.

② Backing-up is very important – for every delivery – but should not be so marked as too risk run-out from the ball played back to the bowler.

③ Of all the means of dismissal, a run-out irks a batsman the most. Once there has been a call of 'yes', both players must commit themselves to the run.

● *The Quick Single: Australia v. England, Texaco Trophy, Trent Bridge, 1989*

England are one up in this series after victory by 95 runs at Old Trafford and here they win the toss and bat, making 226 for five in their 55 overs.

As the last over of the Australian reply begins, they need seven runs to win with their wicket-keeper, Healy, and May at the wicket.

DeFreitas begins the over with a wide and Healy and May take singles from each of the next four balls. Two runs are needed from two balls but DeFreitas bowls May.

The final delivery beats Rackerman and flies through to 'keeper Rhodes standing back but Healy, the non-striker, shows good sense by taking the only option open to him, rushing through for the single as Rhodes throws at, and misses, the stumps.

This single ties the score but England win by virtue of having lost fewer wickets. Healy's quick thinking, however, gave his side a chance. Had Rhodes' throw been especially wild or misfielded, then the Australians might still have snatched victory.

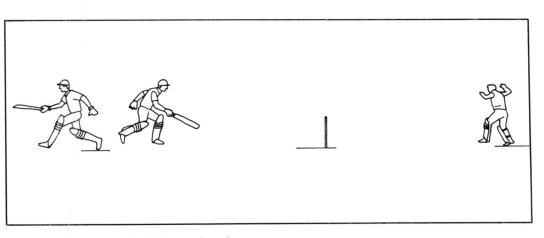

A run can be attempted as the ball passes through to the keeper.

Playing the Short-Pitched Delivery Defensively

● The Tactic

The defensive shot on the back foot to a short ball is the most difficult stroke to play with safety but it is a vital component of a successful batsman's game.

By definition, the bowler will expend more energy in producing a short, lifting ball and for him to see it effectively defended is the ideal riposte for the batsman. If he sees little chance of success with shorter deliveries he will surely have to use other strategies which may be easier to score from.

● Learning the Tactic

① The shot is played by watching first the length of the ball – where it pitches – and then the line it is travelling on.

② From the normal stance, the shot is played with standard backlift and the right foot stepping back in line with the ball.

③ The weight must be chiefly on the ball of the back foot and the angle of the bat controlled by the top hand.

● The Tactic in Use

① If the batsman does not get his back foot in line his whole approach to the shot is wrong, he begins to reach for the ball, and loses control of the bat.

② The top hand must reach up and stay in front so as to slant the bat backwards and direct the ball down.

③ The movement to get in position need not commit the player to the shot. If the ball veers to either side of the wicket he can hold his stance and keep the bat out of the line of the ball.

● *Playing the Short-Pitched Delivery Defensively:*
Robin Smith, England v. West Indies, Headingley, 1988

England's Robin Smith has developed into one of the world's best and most stylish back foot players. Against the West Indies he regularly shows the courage born of the necessity to protect himself after being hit on numerous occasions.

Smith's 38 in the first innings of a match which the West Indies win by ten wickets, is the second best in England's miserly total. Smith is bombarded by short deliveries, especially from Curtly Ambrose, but he remembers the fundamentals of his back foot defensive shot at all times; he gets in line, keeps his back foot parallel with the crease and his front elbow high, his head is still, his eyes on the ball and, most importantly, his bat is kept angled downwards to avoid giving a catch.

The series is to be generally successful for Smith against whom the West Indies' attack find their most potent weapon is seldom successful.

The back foot defensive shot; rear foot in line with the ball and at right angles to the path of the ball.

Attacking the Short-Pitched Delivery

● The Tactic

Once the short ball is misdirected the batsman can look to attack it. If its track is outside off stump then the late cut, square cut or forcing back-foot drive become possible; if it lacks pace or lift, or veers legside, then the pull or hook come into play.

Scoring from the shorter ball is an even more effective way of dissuading the bowler to use it than defending it and it is often the case that the field setting is not placed to cover attacking shots to this bowling. Certainly the area between cover and mid-off is likely to be sparsely defended.

● Learning the Tactic

① The attacking shot cannot be played from the wrong position. The basic movements are as for the defensive shot.

② Power is added to the shot by increasing the length or speed of the downswing of the bat.

③ A full follow-through of the stroke adds to pace and direction and, as opposed to the defensive shot, the bottom hand now plays an equal role.

● The Tactic in Use

① Even the finest player will not always bowl his short deliveries straight. Defend the ones that are; attack the ones which are not.

② Though the initial movement matches that for the defensive shot, the attacking shot may require the batsman to adjust his feet. If he does not stay in line with the ball – eyes and feet – he will lose his balance and become too 'chest on', forcing him to hit across the line.

③ When aiming in front of the wicket, the batsman must make contact with the ball in front of the line of his pads but without reaching for it.

● Attacking the Short-Pitched Delivery: Clive Lloyd, West Indies v. Australia, World Cup Final, Lord's, 1975

Of all his great innings, this 102 in the first World Cup Final is perhaps Clive Lloyd's greatest.

Dennis Lillee, Jeff Thomson and Gary Gilmour are bowling flat out and have three top West Indian batsmen out for 50 when Lloyd ambles to the crease. At lunch he is 34 and his team has recovered to 91 for three from 28 overs. He reaches his 50 off 32 balls and continues his assault on Max Walker. In eight overs after lunch, Lloyd and Rohan Kanhai add 73 runs.

Lloyd's forcing shots on the back foot off Lillee are memorable. The West Indies captain scythes his bat down through the short-pitched balls and follows through majestically, with hands high, as ball after ball is crashed through the field.

His century comes from his 82nd ball and he is then caught behind off Gilmour. Having saved his side, Lloyd watches them amass 291 and bowl out Australia for 274 to become cricket's first World Champions.

The Caribbean back foot drive.

Overcoming the Fear of Fast Bowling

● The Tactic

Fast bowling is the scourge of today's batsman – and there is no sign of any let-up!

In top class cricket, fast bowling has undone the very best batsmen, indeed Graeme Hick, a player of undoubted talent, is currently struggling to maintain his international career after his lacklustre performances against the West Indies in 1991 suggested a fallibility which every quality paceman has since sought to exploit.

It is imperative that batsmen overcome their fear before they attempt to play shots against fast bowling and this can only come from confidence which, in turn, can only be created from a faith in one's ability to deal with pace by tactical awareness and technical correctness.

● Learning the Tactic

① Shock tactics call for shock remedies! Have a team-mate stand ten yards away and throw the ball directly at your head. Start in a batting stance, but without a bat, and catch the ball as it reaches you, ducking your head out of the way only in the moment the ball arrives and a safe catch is made.

② The back foot is crucial in the playing of fast bowling. It must move towards the line on which the ball is arriving so as to get the body in line.

● The Tactic in Use

① The batsman who gets in line to fast bowling retains the option of playing most shots; if you step away or reach for the ball then few safe attacking shots are available and even defence is risky.

② To the shorter ball, the hook or pull is often used. For this the back foot must go further across to the off side.

③ The batsman who has got in line to a fast delivery will be better placed to glance safely on both sides of the wicket, using the pace of the ball to make the scoring shot.

● Overcoming the Fear of Fast Bowling: Allan Border, Australia v. West Indies, Port of Spain, 1983/4

Border has suffered at the hands of Joel Garner in earlier games and in this match the West Indian giant is bowling better and faster than ever after accusations that his career may be nearing its end. Border comes to the wicket with his team 16 for three with Garner having taken all three.

Kim Hughes is caught just before lunch when Australia are 55 for 4 from 16 overs and there is no more play until Saturday morning when the home side concentrate on removing Border. Dean Jones hits 100 in 159 minutes and Australia reach 248 for eight, with Border 92 not out, by the close of the day.

Alderman is last man in next day when Border has progressed to 98. Garner repeatedly beats the Australian skipper but it is Alderman who is dismissed, leaving Border two short of a deserved century.

Border has shown great courage in the face of very hostile bowling and does so again in the second innings when he achieves his century (with Garner off the field). By the end of the drawn match he has batted unbeaten for 630 minutes against furious bowling and dispelled any doubt about his ability to master pace attacks.

Even shorter batsmen can drive pace bowling if the front foot is well forward and the head down.

Driving the Ball

● The Tactic

It is said that if a batsman cannot drive then he is not a complete batsman and will soon lose the initiative to a bowler who notices the weakness and can pitch the delivery accordingly.

The drive allows a batsman to use his full strength, attack the bad ball and hasten his dominance over a bowler.

Even a good length ball from a slow bowler can be driven if the batsman is fast enough on his feet to move down the wicket and hit the ball on the half-volley.

It is the driven shot which a batsman can best direct clear of fielders since he should be fully in command of the shot and be able to place it where there are gaps in the field.

● Learning the Tactic

① Since the nets are for the training of both bowlers and batsmen, the former should be prepared to 'feed' their colleagues half-volleys of varying speeds so the shot can be practised.

② Provided his aim remains to protect his wicket, a batsman can move towards a delivery to make it of driveable length. To practise the foot movement required, put the bat to one side and walk forward into the ball to 'pad' it away as it pitches.

③ When moving into the drive, the final stance when the ball is struck must be as firm and correct as a shot in the crease. Feet must be on the right line, head still and over the ball, and the backlift and follow-through straight and firm.

● The Tactic in Use

① The ineffective or faulty drive is most often seen when the front foot does not get alongside the ball as it pitches. This usually sees the ball lofted and misdirected.

② The front foot drive to a fielder may still produce runs by virtue of the fact that the striker is moving forward as he plays the ball and therefore in a prime position to take the first run.

③ As in golf, the head must be kept down when driving. Allow yourself occasionally to practise the shot with the head lifted and see how difficult it is to play it adequately.

● Driving the Ball: Chris Broad, England v. Australia, Perth, 1986/7

Man-of-the-series Chris Broad opens the innings with Bill Athey with a stand of 233 in which the tall left-hander demonstrates great driving power.

Several England players struggle against the left-arm paceman Bruce Reid but Broad relishes the more natural angle that Reid presents to him. Several times he strides into position to drive the good length ball, exuding confidence as he moves to his highest Test score.

His driving style has him holding his head firm and his wrists flexible as he uses his full height and reach to get the front shoulder and right foot thrust forward at the ball.

England make 592 for eight in their first innings for this drawn match.

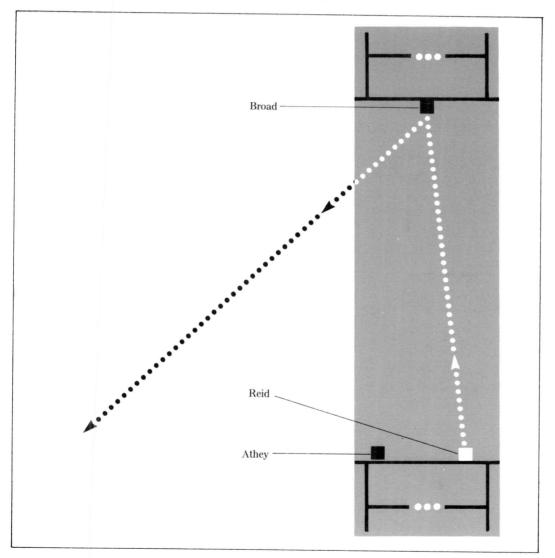

Broad

Reid

Athey

▶ England wicket-keeper, Bob Taylor completes a run-out in a 1979 World Cup match with New Zealand. When the batsmen are as hopelessly out of their ground as they are here, the sole risk to the fielding side is undue haste and an inaccurate throw. The fact that the celebrating bowler is wearing a cap confirms that it is Geoff Boycott during a rare bowling stint. (Colorsport)

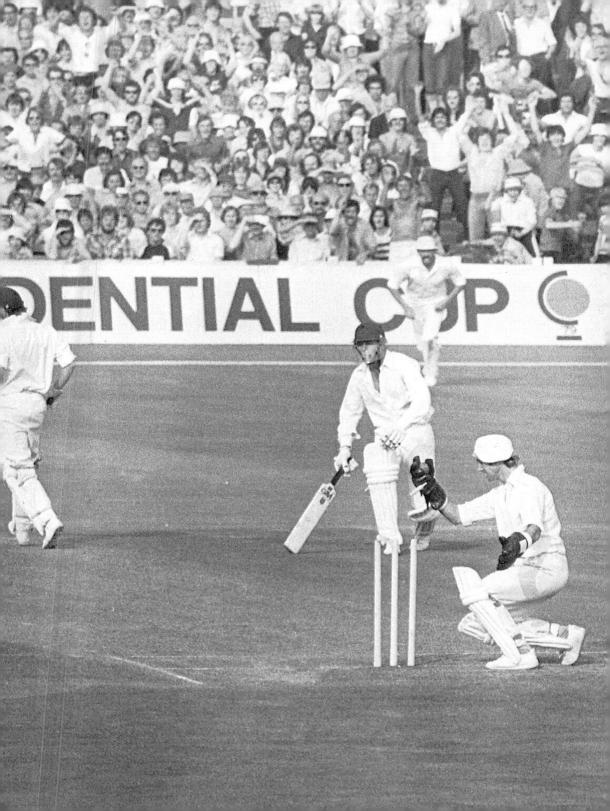

The Cut and the Glance

● The Tactic

As part of his armoury a batsman requires to place his shots where there are fewer fielders or in directions the fielding side find less easy to predict. The square and late cut and the leg glance are very helpful in this respect but can only be played in certain circumstances. Furthermore, in overusing them a batsman is surely failing to play other, more useful, strokes.

The pitch must have bounce and pace before a batsman should consider these shots because he will be using both to direct the ball off an angled bat. These strokes can cause trouble if attempted on a slow, low wicket; the result is more likely to produce a wicket through playing-on or being caught off a leading edge.

The cut is played to a ball outside the line of the off stump which is pitched short to bounce above stump height. The glance can be played off the back foot to a similar ball on the leg-side or to the pitched-up delivery on or outside leg stump.

● Learning the Tactic

① The decision to play the cut comes from reading both the length and line of the delivery; the glance requires the batsman to concentrate chiefly on the line.

② For the cut the batsman, already having moved his back foot towards the line of the ball, will see the ball moving wider

still, move the foot further across and ensure he then judges the bounce so as to strike the ball downwards.

③ For the leg glance, the batsman should practise moving his right foot back and across his crease with his left foot becoming the pivot on which he turns. The left hand will control the bat until the last moment when the other is used to control the final touch on the ball.

● The Tactic in Use

① The common faults in playing these strokes are the failure to keep the cut down and the tendency to flick at the legside ball. Both shots are played off the face of the bat.

② The wider the delivery the further the back foot needs to move across for the cut.

● The Cut and the Glance: Gordon Greenidge, West Indies v. England, Antigua, 1990

Greenidge is acknowledged by most to have been the master of the square cut. In this match the home team, still smarting from an unexpected defeat in the First Test, make sure the fifth game goes their way by dismissing the tourists for 260. Greenidge and Haynes then open with a stand of 298 in a near-perfect display of batting in which Greenidge reaches his century off 134 balls, including 11 fours and two sixes.

Here Greenidge is facing David Capel. The previous delivery has been overpitched and despatched for six but now the bowler over-compensates and pitches marginally too short and wide. Greenidge judges line and length quickly, gets into position and cracks the ball square for another boundary and the West Indies move to 180 for nought.

The forceful square drive; wrist and shoulder power linked with the pace of the ball.

The Game Situation

● The Tactic

The bowler, together with his captain, must be constantly assessing what form the bowling attack will take in a specific game situation. If containment is required then he must bowl defensively to a field he has set; if wickets are a greater priority than runs then he must select his means of attack and pursue them, again with a field set in accordance with the plan.

Throughout the game, but particularly when the match is finely balanced, the bowler must concentrate on the task before him, even to the point of watching how the batsmen are playing his team-mates; loss of concentration, or a lack of appreciation of the game situation, can lose a match.

● Learning the Tactic

① A bowler must learn how to contain a batsman; the batsmen in his team should use net practice to show him where he should pitch the ball to make it difficult for them to score.

② If a batsman is favouring a particular shot the bowler must remove the option by changing his line or length; if the batsman is looking to attack every ball then the bowler must avoid delivering half-volleys and other balls that can be attacked.

● The Tactic in Use

① Bowling is a trial of wits with the two batsmen. A bowler who thinks quicker than the opposition and bowls the ball he wants to will be master of this confrontation.

② Though the ball is with the bowler and only he can put it into play, he must take the advice of experienced team members who are also watching the match situation.

● The Game Situation: Kent v. Middlesex, Benson & Hedges Cup Final, Lord's, 1986

Defending a modest total of 199, Middlesex have to bowl economically throughout the Kent innings. After 13 overs Kent are 20 for three but recover with the help of 58 off 70 balls by Graham Cowdrey.

Kent are left needing 19 from the last twelve balls but suffer a setback when Edmonds bowls Ellison and the last over is reached with 14 runs still needed. Hughes bowls to Marsh who misses the first ball, takes two off the second and flays the third into the Grandstand for six. With just six required from three balls the fourth ball becomes crucial and proves the turning point.

Hughes fires in a near-yorker to Marsh's ankles and the batsman does well to protect his wicket. Though he scrambles a single off the next delivery, Dilley can only manage

two off the last ball so Middlesex, whose bowlers had kept the game situation in their minds all through the Kent innings, win the day.

Balls pitched in the black square make it difficult to make a scoring shot but a minor error, with the ball pitching in the shaded areas, creates half-volleys and full tosses.

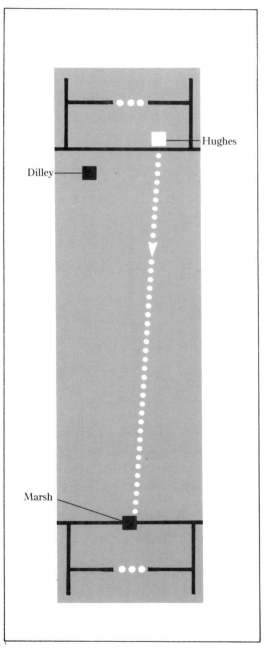

Assessing the Batsman

● *The Tactic*

Bowlers at any level will improve their performance by learning to assess the strengths and weaknesses of the opponents they bowl to . . . and they will enjoy the game more for having done so. In all levels of the game, cricketers tend to play each other year after year and a great deal of useful knowledge can be carried on from one game to another.

As soon as a batsman takes guard, the bowler should begin his assessment, even if he is yet to be asked to bowl. He should look at the grip, the favoured shot, the delivery which causes most problems, and even the mental state of the player − a nervous batsman can be given more pressure by close field placings or a positive player by deliberate containment for his first overs.

● *Learning the Tactic*

① Look at your own players in the nets. Study their grips and the shots they favour because of the way they hold the bat; see if they naturally cut at wide balls, or hook at every short delivery. Once you have assessed the players you already know, you will find it easier to judge new batsmen.

② In net practice, bowlers should seek to bowl continually the type of delivery a colleague does *not* want to receive − both parties will benefit as a result!

● *The Tactic in Use*

① A bowler should take every opportunity to assess a batsman so that it becomes second nature.

② It is always worth taking a second opinion; you may have misread a fault or others may have an alternative means of attacking it.

③ Batsmen's weakness and strengths can extend beyond the shots they play. They may take the first run slowly, or be prone to try for a second run too often.

● *Assessing the Batsman: Curtly Ambrose, West Indies v. England, Edgbaston, 1991*

Graeme Hick finally achieves his aim of playing international cricket for England in the 1991 season, but it is a baptism of fire; ferocious, short-pitched West Indian bowling finds him out and it is a successful tactic born of careful assessment of the new man's strengths and weaknesses.

In the Edgbaston Test Hick bats for a tortuous 147 minutes, facing 104 balls and scoring nineteen. There are a few signs, however, that he is learning to cope with the fierce pace of the West Indian attack − Curtly Ambrose excepted! His first innings is brought to an end when he is caught at slip by Richards off Ambrose.

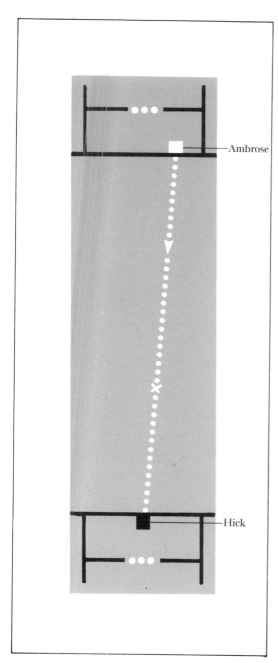

In his second knock the Zimbabwean is at the crease for just eight balls before being clean bowled by Ambrose to make England five for three! It is no commentary on his bravery or determination that the new man, in watching for the shorter ball of which he is so wary, is fooled by a viciously fast Ambrose delivery which is of good length and rips through his defences.

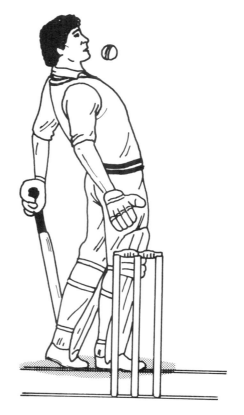

The batsman on the back foot to a short, lifting delivery should still be able to get in line and then duck or sway back out of danger.

Placing the Field and Bowling to it

● The Tactic

The type of bowler, the strengths of the batsmen, the state of the game and the condition of the pitch all have a bearing on field placing – but all the thought and planning applied to it can count for nought if the bowler cannot bowl the ball as required to make the placements effective.

A bowler, and his captain, will need to decide whether to place a field to cover a batsman's favoured shot or seek to bowl in a manner which stops him playing it. Similarly, they may choose to set a deep field for the attacking batsman who lofts the ball or put fielders close in for a new or tentative player.

Whatever decision is taken, the bowler must be aware of the positions of his team-mates at all times and be ready to ask for unorthodox field placings if he feels he can bowl to suit them.

● Learning the Tactic

① Though a bowler should not place his field for his bad deliveries, he has to recognise an ability in a batsman to play a favourite shot. Having seen it played, he is right to 'plug the gap.'

② Bowlers and captains must understand that team-mates may have favourite fielding positions, and encourage specialisation. It is no help to anyone to have someone of slow reaction at slip or your least mobile player in the covers.

③ Once a field is placed, there is no harm in the bowler deliberately offering a ball to be hit if the result might be that the batsman is tempted to offer a catch, but such tactics should be discussed with the captain.

● The Tactic in Use

① Some players have the tendency to move from the position they have been put in. Captains and bowlers should watch for this.

② A bowler must realise the depressing effect bad field placing, or the failure to bowl to the field set, can have on colleagues.

③ Many bowlers and captains tend to change their fields too often; this suggests a lack of thought in the first place or bad bowling!

● Placing the Field and Bowling to it: Merv Hughes, Australia v. England, Headingley, 1989

Australian captain Allan Border gives his

bowlers most of the final day of this match to bowl their opponents out. The target of 408 runs at 4.8 an over is never challenged by England but this should enable their top batsmen to concentrate on defending and holding out for a draw.

The Australians achieve their aim, however, dismissing the home side for 191. Without the challenge of an attacking run chase, the visitors set the fields *they* want and Hughes and Alderman bowl magnificently to them.

Here, wicket-keeper Jack Russell soon succumbs to a short-pitched ball bowled across him in the direction of a close-set 'umbrella' field and is caught by his opposite number, Healy.

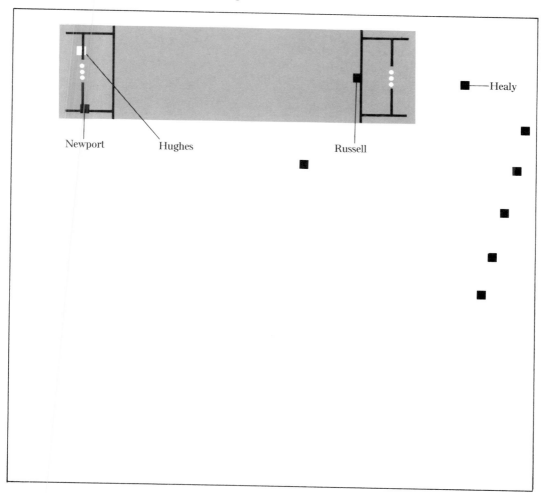

Newport   Hughes   Russell   Healy

Fielding Off Your Own Bowling

● The Tactic

The matter of fielding to your own bowling is all too often omitted from coaching manuals but can be a rewarding tactic which can be deliberately employed, rather than simply being considered a question of quick reaction when the need arises.

Whether or not a bowler fields well to his own bowling will certainly depend largely on his agility, reflexes and reactions but, properly thought through, his actions can give his side eleven genuine fielders. For example, a short extra cover may well be able to be relocated if a bowler takes it upon himself to cover the shot played there.

The dismissal of 'caught and bowled' may well be most often brought about by a mis-hit shot but no-one will get an earlier or clearer view of a stroke played in the 'V' than the bowler and he should try to watch for chances to act as bowler *and* fielder.

● Learning the Tactic

① Bowlers should train themselves to keep their eye on the ball throughout their follow-through. Many find their action sometimes forces them to miss the actual shot being played.

② They should also practise the quick pick-up and throw, as part of their follow-through.

③ By making it clear that he is actively looking to field from his own bowling, a player will discourage the running of quick singles from pushed shots in front of the wicket.

● The Tactic in Use

① Of all the fielding side, the bowler will get the first indication that a delivery is going to be played back towards him. He should therefore be able to react quicker than anyone.

② There will always be a gap in the field behind the bowler. If the ball passes him he should immediately call the nearest fielder to chase the ball.

● Fielding Off Your Own Bowling: Ian Botham, England v. Pakistan, 1987

In a match which, by his own high standards, does not see him at his best, Ian Botham still manufactures a wicket by superb reactions and athleticism.

Salem Malik has hit four boundaries in his 17 when he drives Botham back down the wicket. Though into his follow-through which is taking him in the opposite direction, the all-rounder turns quickly to catch the ball

in his right hand before tumbling to the ground.

Malik has not played a particularly bad shot. He only just fails to keep the drive on the ground but his error is fatal because of Botham's competitive alertness and his determination to take every opportunity of a wicket.

The right-arm bowler should look to 'control' the pitch area shown.

41

▲ Viv Richards joins his West Indian colleagues in a pre-match fitness programme. Such is the pace of the modern game at all levels, fitness requirements are so much greater and a player leaves himself open to injury if he does not properly prepare for the season, and then for each game. (Colorsport)

▶ The slip cordon, alert and ready for the edged shot. Boycott, Miller, Gooch, Hendrich, Brearley and Taylor wait in eager anticipation and will stay crouched until the ball is played; if the edge comes low they are better placed to reach it from this position. (Colorsport)

The Bouncer

● The Tactic

There has been more controversy about the bowling of bouncers in recent years than any other aspect of the game on the pitch. For many spectators, however, there is nothing to compare with the spectacle of a good bouncer dismissing a good batsman.

The key ingredient of the effective bouncer is surprise; as a bad bouncer can be a wasted ball so a good bouncer should not be able to be anticipated by the batsman.

A bouncer usually pitches in an area similar to the long hop and lifts towards the upper body. It is arguable whether the bouncer has a place in the lesser ranks of the amateur game – the batsman facing it will have to go to work on Monday! – but it is difficult to dissuade a pace bowler at any level to refrain from using it if he has the ability to deliver it.

● Learning the Tactic

① All too often a fast bowler allows himself, or is allowed, to strive for pace before accuracy. In truth, the best bouncer is very deliberate and accurate and cannot be regularly bowled if the user relies on unthinking brute force.

② Strength and fitness are prerequisites for the bowler aiming to deploy the bouncer.

③ In his net practice a fast bowler must learn where he has to pitch the ball to produce an accurate bouncer; it is a very precise spot.

● The Tactic in Use

① Using the bouncer too often will remove the surprise factor and risk physical injury to the bowler.

② Bouncers do not produce wickets by hitting the batsman, but by having him play an awkward, involuntary shot.

● The Bouncer: Michael Holding, West Indies v. England, The Oval, 1984

In this final Test the visitors complete a 5–0 series victory despite Garner and Marshall suffering from stomach cramps during England's second innings. They rely on Michael Holding to reproduce some of his old firepower.

In gloomy conditions Holding glides to the wicket with his usual grace and rhythm which camouflages his awesome pace and power. To Gower he somehow conjures up more effort and releases the ball a fraction later so as to pound it into the hard Oval track.

When on 14, Gower receives a delivery from Holding which has the length and line which demands it be played at but it bites into the pitch, lifts and clips off the gloves of

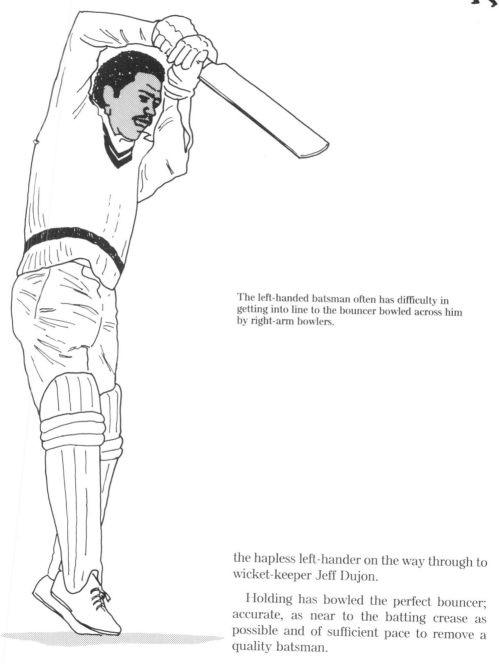

The left-handed batsman often has difficulty in getting into line to the bouncer bowled across him by right-arm bowlers.

the hapless left-hander on the way through to wicket-keeper Jeff Dujon.

Holding has bowled the perfect bouncer; accurate, as near to the batting crease as possible and of sufficient pace to remove a quality batsman.

The Yorker

● The Tactic

The yorker is the ball which pitches at the batsman's feet and can be extremely effective if bowled with an added injection of pace. As with the bouncer, the yorker should be used as a surprise tactic and if over-used it will simply persuade a batsman to change his position at the crease to make such a delivery into a half-volley or full toss.

A bowler should be watching for opportunities to use this tactical delivery. For a new batsman it is always worthwhile to bowl a yorker as he will have arrived at the wicket expecting standard deliveries and with a policy to defend them. Other times to use the yorker may be for batsmen with high back-lifts, directly after a series of shorter deliveries or when the batsman may be expecting a shorter ball, and to the player who has a tendency to move outside the leg stump when playing his shots.

● Learning the Tactic

① In bowling the yorker, the player has little margin for error; accuracy is everything. Try marking a circle the size of a large dinner plate with the edge of the circle just covering the popping crease and its centre in line with the space between middle and off stumps.

② When using this training routine also make a similar mark where a well directed standard ball should pitch so that five

balls can be aimed there, followed by the 'surprise' delivery of yorker length.

③ Though it is more difficult for the spin bowler to use the yorker, he should still practise it and use it when he can.

● The Tactic in Use

① The bowler, and his captain, must understand the risk in bowling an inaccurate yorker; if it becomes a full toss or half-volley it may be punished. Do not use it unless you are confident of your accuracy.

② If a batsman successfully defends a yorker he will still find it difficult to score from; it is, therefore, a good containing tactic if bowled well.

● The Yorker: Michael Holding, West Indies v. England, The Oval, 1976

All the great West Indian bowlers, as well as being superb exponents of the bouncer, have been masters of delivering a yorker.

In this example, Michael Holding bowls Tony Greig for just one run in the second innings of a match in which he is to take 14 wickets. The West Indian knew that Greig had a high backlift, he might claim to have invented the style, so he produces a perfect

yorker of extra pace which rips through the tall man's defences, removes his middle and leg stumps and sets back England's cause still further.

The West Indies win the match by 231 runs.

A. The batsman with a high backlift may be found susceptible to the yorker. B. With extra pace the yorker can beat the downward stroke.

The Googly

● *The Tactic*

As the bouncer and yorker are the secret weapons in the pace bowler's armoury, so the googly is the leg-spinner's surprise package. The googly is an off-break bowled with a leg-break action to a right-handed batsman.

This delivery is considered the most subtle of all cricket's arts involving, as it does, the bowler screwing the ball out of his hand over a cocked wrist.

Whilst the technique may not be so confusing to a batsman who chooses not to read the spinner's intention 'from his hand', the effect of the ball turning off the wicket in the opposite direction to that which the batsman is expecting is bound to have even a quality player in trouble.

● *Learning the Tactic*

① Of all the bowling techniques this requires the most practice. It needs the bowler to have supple wrists and fingers.

② Grip and delivery action are fundamental. The simplest grip is with the second and third fingers spread to grip the ball with the third wedged alongside the seam.

③ Two wrist actions are required to bowl the googly: first, the ball must travel over the wrist on the little finger side of the hand. Then the delivery should be led by the bent wrist which is dropped to allow the ball to flip over.

● *The Tactic in Use*

① The secret is in the fact that the back of the hand faces the batsman. The wrist turns over earlier than for leg spin which means the batsman has no sight of the ball at the point of delivery.

② As with all surprise tactics, a leg spinner cannot practise the delivery during the game. If he finds he has become 'rusty' and inaccurate he must discontinue bowling it until he can practise more.

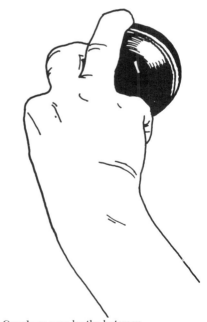

The Googly as seen by the batsman.

● The Googly:
Abdul Qadir, Pakistan v.
England, Karachi, 1984

Qadir arrived on the international cricket scene like a breath of fresh air and it was the rarity of facing leg spin of his quality which had the world's leading players in constant trouble.

For most of this match the England batsmen have no idea which way the ball will turn. Not one of them can honestly claim to be able to read the bowler's intentions from his hand.

In the first innings Qadir dismisses Botham with a googly. Earlier leg breaks from the spinner had ended up in line with the slip fielder and, receiving the 'wrong 'un', the Englishman is caught by Rameez Raja at backward short-leg for 22.

Asked at what stage he had 'picked' the googly, Botham replied, 'When it fetched up in short-leg's hands.'

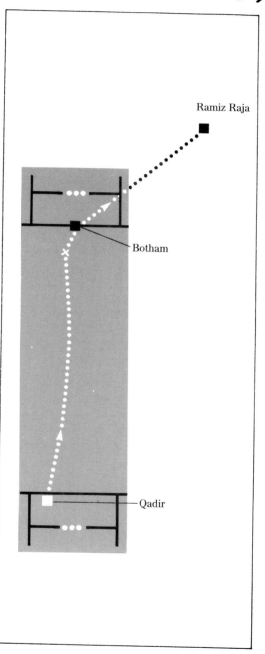

Variation in Pace, Flight and Angle

● The Tactic

By varying pace, the angle of attack and the flight of the ball, a thinking bowler of average ability can greatly improve his figures.

Different degrees of flight cause problems because every batsman makes a guess at the angle of descent of every ball he receives and if he is fooled by a change of flight he will misjudge the length.

Both slow and fast bowlers can vary pace with effective results; the spinner can quickly learn to disguise a faster ball and, whilst it is harder for a paceman suddenly to deliver a slower ball from the same action, even a subtle alteration in pace can induce a false shot.

The angle of attack can disrupt a batsman's confidence, giving him yet another factor to watch for in each delivery.

● Learning the Tactic

① Variations must be disguised as well as possible. Suddenly veering away to bowl from wide on the crease merely forewarns the batsman.

② Similarly, the spin bowler must practise delivering his faster ball by simply bringing his front foot down harder, pivoting more fully and accelerating the final stage of his delivery.

● The Tactic in Use

① The simplest means of changing angle is to move from bowling over the wicket to round the wicket. A change of field may be required.

② Adjust your field positions several balls before you vary your attack so as to avoid signalling your intentions.

③ The wicket-keeper should be forewarned of your intentions if possible.

● Variation in Pace, Flight and Angle: Bob Massie, Australia v. England, Lord's, 1972

In the most remarkable debut in the history of Test cricket, Bob Massie finishes with figures of 16 for 137 and, not surprisingly, the game becomes known as 'Massie's Test'.

Here he bowls four successive outswingers to Basil D'Oliveira. Each starts its flight apparently targetted at middle stump but late in its flight veers sharply away outside off stump. The Worcestershire player is having to watch every delivery like a hawk, trying desperately to decide which ball he has to play and which he can leave alone.

The next ball begins marginally wider and the batsman can begin to plan an attacking

shot to a ball which, based on the preceding quartet, will swing wide of off-stump. This ball, however, suddenly takes a new line, ducking in to the stumps, rather than away, and D'Oliveira is trapped LBW having been unable to alter his shot.

John Snow was amongst those who claimed Massie's swing bowling was unlike any they had ever seen before.

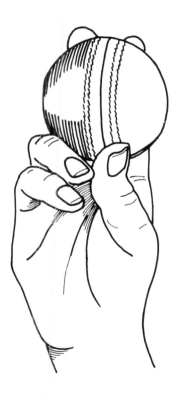

The grip for the inswinger.

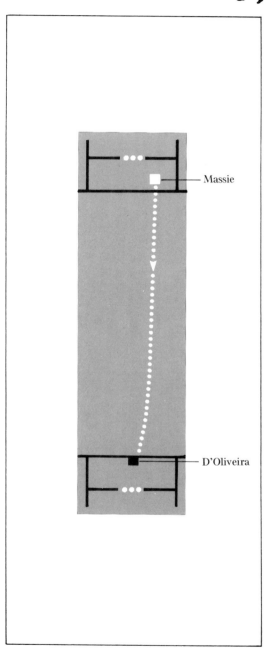

Massie

D'Oliveira

Captaining in the Field

● The Tactic

The captain should lead his side with an optimistic approach, with a readiness to encourage his colleagues at every opportunity. He must be a good motivator and appreciate that there is more to his job than winning the toss!

He will have to do the thinking for at least some of his players and is likely to be the one to give most thought to the opposition. He must have considered the strengths and weaknesses of the opponents and have some plans to deal with them. He should also have an idea of how he will use his own players, particularly his bowlers, though such plans will need to be adaptable.

The best captains are those who are, at all times, confident, assertive without being aggressive, and capable of backing personal judgement.

● Learning the Tactic

① Captains need to be tactically alert so as to guide their players at times when strategic thinking is called for. This does not suit all players; many prefer to concentrate only on their game and thus do not make good captains.

② Captains should build a knowledge of their opposition, from previous matches or from the current game as it progresses, so as to suggest tactical action to teammates.

③ A captain must be efficient in the placing of a field and be ready to adapt it according to the bowler, batsman, pitch and atmospheric conditions and the state of the game.

● The Tactic in Use

① A captain must think on his feet, reacting quickly to changes in the match. His vice-captain and other senior players can help.

② Without contributing with a major personal performance with bat or ball, a captain can still turn a game, even win it.

③ A captain has to understand colleagues needs; some require gentle encouragement whilst others need more vigorous demonstrations of support.

● Captaining in the Field: Mike Brearley, England v. Australia, Headingley, 1981

Ian Botham has resigned as Captain after 12 Tests without a win and the selectors recall Mike Brearley, one of the most remarkable skippers of all time.

In this Third Test Australia bat first and score 401, with Botham taking six wickets, and England reply with a paltry 174. Following-on, they lose Gooch without a run on the board but Botham hits a century off 87 balls

and England are 124 ahead at the end of the fourth day.

Early on the last day Australia begin their seemingly easy task of making 130 to win and, at 56 for two, are almost home.

Now Brearley changes Bob Willis to the end where he will have the strong wind at his back. The tall paceman is transformed and takes eight wickets for 43 off 15.1 overs to clinch an unlikely English victory by 18 runs.

Brearley has not only become the first captain to lead a Test team to victory from a follow-on position but in his handling of Willis and his predecessor, Botham, as well as excellent field placing, has shown leadership skills of the highest order.

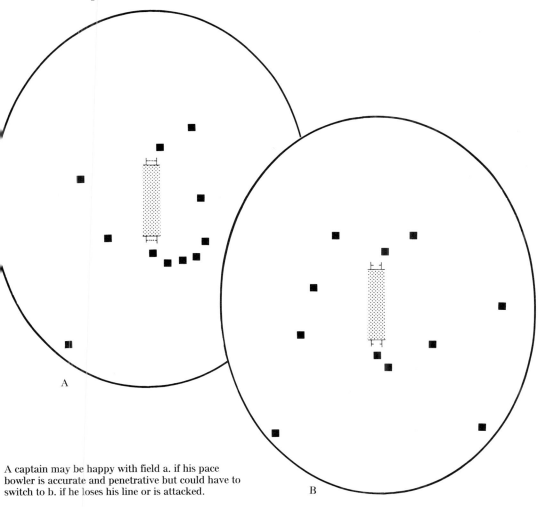

A

B

A captain may be happy with field a. if his pace bowler is accurate and penetrative but could have to switch to b. if he loses his line or is attacked.

▲ His first international season was a rude awakening for Graeme Hick whose vulnerability to fast, accurate short-pitched bowling was exposed by the West Indian attack. For a batsman of such obvious pedigree to have to re-learn the fundamentals of batting technique demonstrates how a cricketer can never claim to have leant it all! (Colorsport)

▶ David Gower is on his toes to defend against Australia at Headingley in 1989. Though suffering from the left-hander's traditional weakness to the ball bowled across him, Gower has still enjoyed a fine international career and earned a reputation for stylish batting of the highest class. (Colorsport)

Wicketkeeping to Slow Bowling

● The Tactic

Apart from the Captain, the wicket-keeper is the most valuable member of a fielding side at any level of the game. He is ideally placed to see the movement of the ball and assess the ability of the batsmen. A sensible captain will take note of the advice given by his 'keeper.

When standing up to the stumps for slow bowling the wicket-keeper can exert even greater influence on the game. Apart from the pressure his closeness puts on the batsman, he can also act as a further close-in fieldsman to defensive shots and stop many quick singles. He can also, of course, directly dismiss a batsman if he takes a stumping chance.

● Learning the Tactic

① The wicket-keeper should ensure he can see the delivery from the bowler's hand and avoid the temptation of standing too close to the stumps and so hamper his view.

② He must practise staying in his crouched position as late as possible, rising with the ball after its bounce. As with any close fielder, to rise too soon makes the regaining of low position more difficult.

③ The 'keeper needs to be very fit. Suppleness in the back is vital, as is the spring in the legs, so exercises for these regions are a necessity.

● The Tactic in Use

① The wicket-keeper has to concentrate at the same level as the batsman!

② When he takes the ball the 'keeper should endeavour to have his weight on the foot nearest the wicket so as to increase the speed with which he can make a stumping.

③ The 'keeper should not move to the legside too early or too far before he has picked up the line of the ball.

● Wicketkeeping to Slow Bowling: Alan Knott, England v. West Indies, Lord's, 1976

Equally effective standing back or close to the stumps, Alan Knott evolved a wonderful understanding with his Kent team-mate, Derek Underwood, a left-arm slow-medium bowler who enjoyed great success with England.

For many a club 'keeper, Underwood's pace, faster than the average spinner, would have been sufficient reason to stand a little back from the stumps but Knott took many

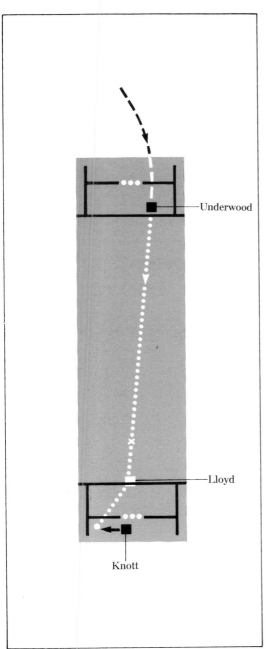

catches and stumpings off him and came to be able to 'read' Underwood's deliveries better than the batsmen facing him.

Here, Clive Lloyd is well set, with a solid half-century to his name, when Underwood – still bowling round the wicket despite Lloyd's left-handed stance – drifts a slower ball across the West Indian, finds the edge and sees Knott use lightning reflexes to capture the half-chance. The angle of the delivery must have made it a difficult ball for Knott to 'read'.

When standing up, the wicketkeeper needs to stay low and rise with the ball.

Wicketkeeping to Pace

● The Tactic

To faster bowlers the wicket-keeper will stand back and may prefer to crouch rather than adopt the full squat position. Whatever stance he takes the 'keeper will find himself having to cover a wide arc and, on lesser wickets, the ball arriving at varying heights.

Catches in this position are usually faint edges where the pace of the ball is barely affected and yet the direction can be dramatically altered. There is no practice like getting actual chances in a match but a 'keeper can hone his reactions by working on a slip catching cradle or by team-mates 'faking' edges during training.

In taking a ball which has passed the bat, the wicket-keeper must first concentrate on catching it safely or, at least, stop it passing him. To avoid damaging his hands he will need to 'give' a little as the ball arrives; the prime exponents of the art are said to have 'soft hands' as they can collect a fast ball without it thudding into rigid gloves.

● Learning the Tactic

① 'Keepers must learn to stand at the right distance from the stumps. Many stand too close for the speed of their reactions; others stand so deep that the ball is dipping to their feet or bouncing before it reaches them.

② Foot movement is most important. 'Keepers should practise shuffling side-

ways to reach the ball so reducing the need to dive and risk missing the ball or having it jarred loose when they hit the ground.

③ Only use the pads to stop the ball in the most dire emergency. It is almost impossible to control the collection of the ball by this means.

● The Tactic in Use

① An efficient wicket-keeper is a major asset and inspires confidence in a team. One who concedes byes or drops catches by standing too close or too deep, or by diving unnecessarily, is a handicap.

② The wicket-keeper must 'own' the pitch within 15 yards of the batsman's crease, acting as an extra fielder, getting to the stumps for throws and possible run outs and generally making the batting side aware of his presence.

③ The 'keeper must concentrate on his own game first but also look to advise his captain on tactical observations he is in the best position to make.

● Wicketkeeping to Pace: Jeff Dujon, West Indies v. England, Lord's, 1984

Jeff Dujon has been an exceptional wicket-keeper for the West Indies, subjected, as he has been, to keeping to the fastest bowlers in the world for many years. He has frequently ended a long day in the field with bruised and cut hands but his supreme technique has limited such damage and his fine fitness and intense concentration kept him at the top of his profession.

A whole book could be written on Dujon's tactical excellence in keeping to the West Indian pacemen. In this Test, he is called upon to take one of the most difficult catches – the legside glance by a left-handed batsman to a right-arm bowler. Dujon has to stand well outside the line of Chris Broad's off stump in order to watch Malcolm Marshall's angled approach and sharp delivery from the centre of the crease. Though Dujon has a split second to notice the ball is directed at leg stump, he has less time to realise the England opener has edged it legside. With a lightning shuffle and an explosive leap, he plucks the ball out of the air.

Standing back, most wicketkeepers prefer to be in the stoop position just after the ball has bounced.

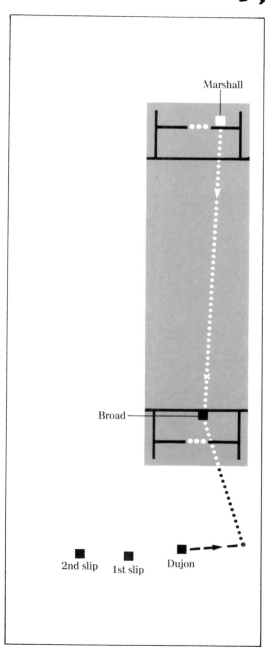

Marshall

Broad

2nd slip

1st slip

Dujon

Slip Fielding

● The Tactic

Slip fielding is a vital part of the game at any level and any club player can make himself a good slip fielder if he has good eyes, quick reactions, concentration and a willingness to keep these qualities keen. The cliché 'catches win matches' is never more true than when applied to the slips and yet many clubs fail to train specialists for this position.

The slip fielder will take his position from the wicket-keeper and must have a good understanding with him; he must also be ready to cover the 'keeper in the event of the ball being only partially stopped.

An efficient slip field is all part of the pressure which can be applied to a batting side. If catches are dropped, edges pass through the cordon for runs or the fielders there are standing too deep, the initiative is handed back to the batsmen.

● Learning the Tactic

① A comfortable stance is essential. The fielder must be able to stoop, dive, jump and hold a straight fast edge from the position he takes.

② This stance must be held with the balance on the balls of the feet and even the threat of a fast edge flying towards him must not drive the fielder back onto his heels, as this will prevent him making rapid moves.

③ Of all fielding positions the slips require the most practice. An hour a week on the slip catching cradle or with team-mates 'faking' edges, will be certain to bring reward.

● The Tactic in Use

① Always catch two-handed if possible. Watch the ball into the hand.

② The eye line is as follows: first and second slip watch the ball from the bowler's hand onto the bat whilst from third slip outwards the fielder should concentrate only on the bat because of the degree of angle.

● Slip Fielding: Clive Lloyd, West Indies v. England, Old Trafford, 1984

There have been some outstanding slip fielders in the history of cricket. In the postwar era Bobby Simpson, Colin Cowdrey, Gary Sobers and Viv Richards have been responsible for some great catches at the highest level. The latter began his Test career as a lightning-quick outfielder before settling for the quieter but equally demanding slip cordon. The same applied to Clive Lloyd who is featured here.

In this one-day international, England's Graeme Fowler, a left-hander, faces the tall Joel Garner bowling right-arm, over the

wicket. He fends at a fast ball directed across him and edges towards Lloyd at first slip. The eager Dujon makes a move for the ball and surely comes into Lloyd's line of vision but the skipper holds his concentration, takes the speeding ball at his left shoulder and is toppled backwards by the impact.

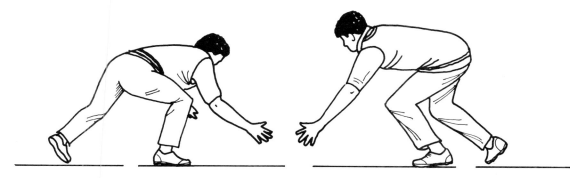

The value in slip fielders staying in the crouch; the low edge can be missed if the fielder has stood up.

Close Catching

● The Tactic

Apart from the slips, other close catching positions include gully, silly point, silly mid-off and mid-on and the short legs. It often seems in today's cricket that fielders are put in these places to intimidate and unsettle the batsman and relatively few catches are taken there.

In club cricket, close fielders are unlikely to wear the protective clothing, boast the same reflexes or benefit from such accurate bowling as their professional counterparts and therefore careful consideration by individuals, and their captain, must be given to the dangers compared to the likely benefits to the team.

Those who do field close must prepare as a slip fielder – a comfortable low stance which is retained until the ball is played. At club level the gully position can be very important and a good fielder there can save runs and take catches.

● Learning the Tactic

① Practice sharpens the all-important reflexes and must be undertaken before every game.

② The stance must provide balance on the balls of the feet. A fielder's reactive moves are slowed if he is back on his heels.

③ Concentration is everything. Watch for where the ball pitches, how the batsman prepares for the shot, and be prepared to turn and chase the ball if it passes you.

● The Tactic in Use

① Close fielders must be aware of their territory, the arc of the pitch they are covering.

② Catches which come via the bat *and* either pads or the batsman's body will travel slower and with a different trajectory.

③ Close catchers can support their bowler and wicket-keeper by covering the stumps for throw-ins and run-out opportunities.

● Close Fielding: David Gower, England v. West Indies, Lord's, 1988

Some of the more gifted cricketers have been quality fielders in a number of positions – Gary Sobers, Clive Lloyd and Allan Lamb, for example. David Gower is another who is equally effective close to the wicket as he is patrolling the covers or mid-wicket area.

In this Test the home team dismiss the visitors for 209 and Curtly Ambrose is one of the last four wickets which fall for just 25 runs. Facing Gladstone Small, he plays a rash shot outside off stump and the ball flashes to gully where Gower takes a fine diving catch.

Gower has watched the ball from the bat, reacted quickly to pick up the line, and caught the ball two-handed when it is almost past him.

The close catching stance. Balance should always be forward on the balls of the feet.

High Catching

● *The Tactic*

Taking a high catch focuses everyone's attention on the player concerned. He may have time to feel the fear of failure as he waits for the ball; he may have to be calling to colleagues to leave the catch to him; he may have to run to get into position. Whatever the case, the high catch which is dropped becomes a very obvious lost opportunity.

Much practice in the art of catching high balls is undertaken in a light-hearted fashion, before a game, rather than with the aim of correcting faults in technique or experimenting with new methods.

● *Learning the Tactic*

① Under a high catch, the fielder should try to get into position to create a firm stance so that he can then use his upstretched hands as 'sights' down which the ball travels into his cupped hands.

② Whether static or running, the fielder must keep his hands flexible so that they can absorb the impact of the ball arriving. The ball will bounce from rigid hands, and bruise them.

③ The baseball-style catch is now popular. Here the 'receiving area' is created by the thumbs being turned knuckle-to-knuckle and the hands cupped in an outward-facing style; traditionally the hands were cupped with the inside of the wrists touching and the elbows tucked into the chest.

● *The Tactic in Use*

① Once the ball is in the air the fielder best placed to take the catch must identify his position to anyone who may impede him.

② Never be persuaded to take your eye off the ball.

③ If the catch is dropped do not delay in returning it to the wicket-keeper and do not risk the double indignity of an inaccurate throw.

● *High Catching: Allan Lamb, England v. Australia, Headingley, 1985*

The best fielders will adopt a two-stage approach to a high catch. They will initially concentrate solely on getting into position and will keep their hands at their sides at this point – test how much more difficult it is to run quickly with your arms out in front of you! Only when they have got in their catching position and the ball is arriving will they cup their hands in their preferred style and take the catch.

From Ian Botham's bowling, Wayne Phillips slices a skied shot towards extra cover. Lamb has to run backwards to get close to the dropping ball and even then still takes the catch above his head. He has kept his eyes on the ball from the moment it has left the bat and cupped his hands at the last possible moment, having got himself into the best position he could.

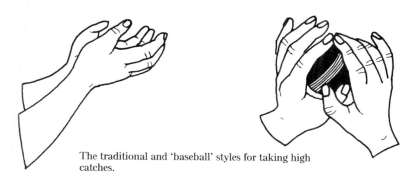

The traditional and 'baseball' styles for taking high catches.

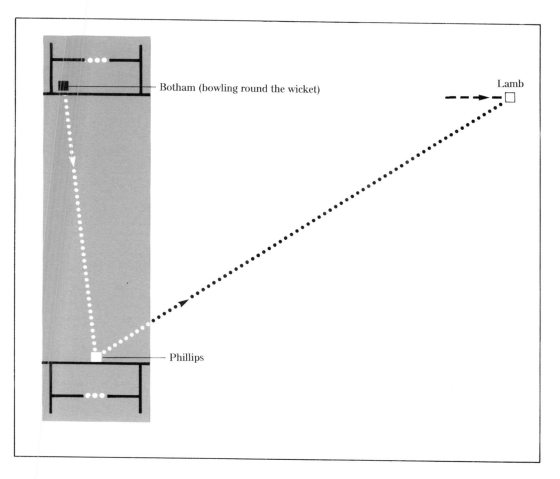

Botham (bowling round the wicket)

Lamb

Phillips

◀ Responsible for some of the most spectacular slip catches of recent years, Ian Botham demonstrates the art here, against the Australians at Trent Bridge in 1989. His eyes are firmly focused on the ball and he has managed to capture it with both hands. (Colorsport)

▲ Graham Gooch faces Terry Alderman in the Test series of 1989 during which the accuracy and success of the Australia pace man caused the English management to invent the description of his bowling "in the corridor of uncertainty". In truth, Alderman got close to the stumps at his end, bowled "wicket to wicket" and, through achieving late swing, persuaded batsmen to play at balls they could have left. (Colorsport)

67

Outfielding

● *The Tactic*

It is said that outfielders should accept the single but allow no other run to be scored. In other words, they should seek to cut off boundaries and cover the field in such a way and at a pace which precludes more than one run being taken.

The key to successful fielding, given good placement by the captain, is to hold your given location and move quickly forward as the ball is bowled. A batsman will often be dissuaded from attempting a run simply because a fielder has, by his anticipation, threatened to make a quick pick up.

Players fielding in the deep should never wait for the rolling ball to reach them unless they are confident the batsmen are only taking a single. When they collect the ball they should not run forward with the ball before throwing it in, just because they want to reach the 'keeper's gloves, but should throw immediately even if that means the ball bouncing before it reaches the wicket-keeper.

● *Learning the Tactic*

① The ground shot should be blocked, if possible, by the hands being placed in front of the widest barrier the player can make. This is usually achieved by bending down on one knee to overlap the other heel, all at right angles to the ball.

② The throw can be made longer and more accurate by better technique. The non-throwing arm is used as the 'sight', the body turned sideways and then pivoted as the throwing arm is brought forward and the ball thrown; the throwing arm following through to point after the ball.

③ Mobility and suppleness are most important and simple exercises should be continued through the game to ensure you are ready to run, stoop and throw without injury.

● *The Tactic in Use*

① Fielders will enjoy their cricket more if they work at improving their fielding; it is what they spend much of every game doing!

② An enthusiastic and efficient fielding side can win a game as readily as good batting and bowling.

③ Outfielders must be ready to support team-mates as the need arises and back-up 'keepers and bowlers fielding incoming throws.

● *Outfielding: Derek Randall, Nottinghamshire v. Northamptonshire, NatWest Trophy Final, Lord's, 1987*

Randall's effervescent behaviour on the cricket pitch has sometimes disguised his mastery of the fielding basics which have made him one of the finest exponents of the art.

In this match he performs several excellent pieces of fielding including a moment where he dashes to retrieve a shot from Wayne Larkins and allows the Northants opener just one run.

Randall exhibits the three principles of fielding excellence:

① head over the ball and his legs creating the broadest possible block to the ball.

② weight on the back foot and his left foot at right angles to the direction of the throw.

③ weight transferred to the front foot with the body pivoting and the back foot brought forward with the impetus of the throw.

Form a broadest obstacle to the ball and follow through with the throwing action to achieve pace and direction.

Throwing

● *The Tactic*

A good, clean throw can save runs, achieve run-outs and put pressure on the batting side.

Efficient throwing means accuracy first, speed second, and both come from sound technique. Inefficiency is caused by undue haste, lack of support from team-mates, and poor technique.

If good throwing is disconcerting for the batting side, the gift of overthrows by bad throwing and backing-up takes pressure off the batsmen and gives them runs they would have otherwise had to work for.

Not every cricketer is capable of a long or fast throw and a thinking batsman will be watching for this. A player must compensate for a weak throw by reacting quickly and, at least, threatening to complete a hard throw.

● *Learning the Tactic*

① Reaching, picking up and preparing to throw the ball are all part of the technique which has to be trained for and perfected. Basic sprinting speed helps and, as ever, it is essential to keep your eye on the ball.

② For both shoulder-level and overarm throws, the right foot is at right angles to the line of the throw.

③ For a long throw, the arm is taken right back but for a quick short throw the arm

should be bent. The quick underarm or flick throw can go badly wrong if the fielder releases the ball too late or is not balanced at the point of the throw.

● *The Tactic in Use*

① The fielder should try to keep aware, as he collects the ball, which end he is best advised to throw to. If he throws to the bowler's end he should be sure someone is covering that area.

② The underarm flick to the 'keeper is difficult for him to collect if it runs along the ground but the throwing hand should not reach too far before releasing the ball as this may cause the throw to lob up over the wicket-keeper's head.

● *Throwing: Devon Malcolm, England v. West Indies, Jamaica, 1990*

In this historic England victory, Devon Malcolm sets up his team with a magnificent throw which precipitates the West Indies collapse.

The home side are 63 without loss in their first innings when Angus Fraser bowls to Gordon Greenidge. The opener, who has scored 32, steers the ball towards Malcolm at long leg and races off for his first run. He turns at the bowler's end with the thought in his mind that Malcolm is not the sharpest fielder but has forgotten that the Englishman has an awesome throw.

Malcolm initially fumbles the ball – supporting Greenidge's opinion of his fielding ability – but recovers quickly to throw accurately to the 'keeper's end to score a direct hit on the stumps.

Greenidge has gambled on Malcolm's fielding weaknesses but a brilliant throw – accurate and powerful – sees him lose the gamble and his wicket.

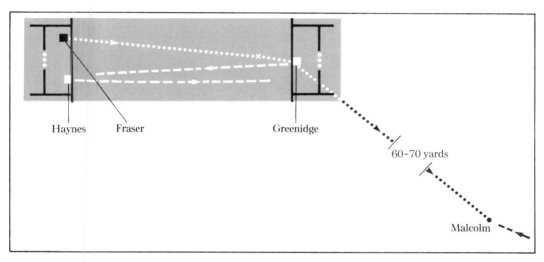

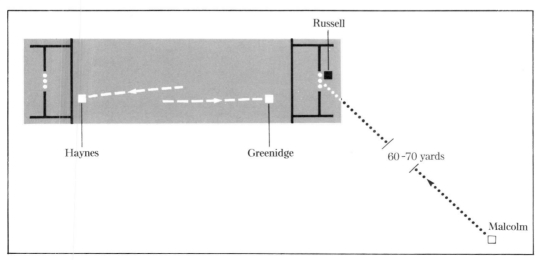

Attacking the Ball

● The Tactic

Runs can be saved by players running towards the ball to field it rather than waiting for it to arrive, by being on the move at the point of delivery so that they can quickly attack the ball which is stroked towards them and by turning quickly and catching the ball which has passed them.

Basic speed and quickness of turn must be added to anticipation and alertness so the serious cricketer has plenty to work on if his fielding is to improve.

If the moving ball can be quickly and safely retrieved and got back into the wicket-keeper's hands the batsman will feel he has to hit boundaries to advance his score significantly.

● Learning the Tactic

① As he is likely to have to field in every position at some time or other, even a close fielding specialist must practise ground work in the outfield.

② When attacking the ball rolling towards you the first requirement is to create a broad defence which will stop the ball. The hands will be placed ahead of the body to collect the ball and the feet then immediately transferred to the throwing stance in order to get rid of the ball quickly.

③ When chasing the ball, the right-handed player will aim to overtake the ball on its left side, allow the ball to run into his right hand and, once it is safely gathered, immediately take up his throwing stance.

● The Tactic in Use

① Watch the ball off the bat and move forward or laterally as soon as you can assess its direction.

② Having made a quick interception the fielder may have occasionally to satisfy himself with that rather than risk over-throws by returning the ball to unattended stumps.

● Attacking the Ball: Philip DeFreitas, England v. West Indies, Lord's, 1991

DeFreitas is one of the finest outfielders in the game. Quick to the ball and with a fast, low throw, he also has the ability to get his return away quickly. He also has excellent anticipation as is shown here in the last England series against the West Indies.

Devon Malcolm follows a short ball to Philip Simmons with one of good length which the tall opener is able to hit soundly off his legs through mid-wicket. DeFreitas, at wide mid-off, has marched forward as the ball is bowled and now watches the ball from the bat. He flings himself to the right and stops the ball with his fingertips so keeping Simmons to one run when he must have been expecting three or even a boundary four.

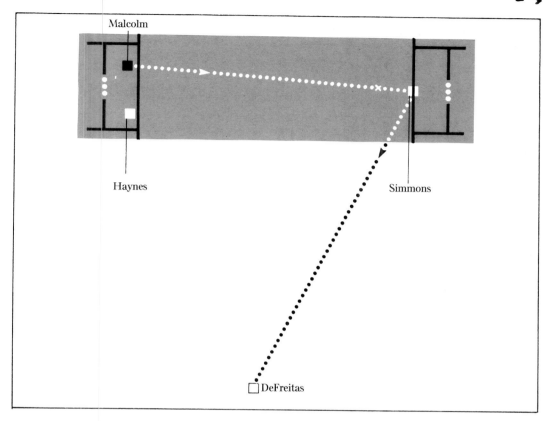

Malcolm

Haynes

Simmons

DeFreitas

Eyes on the ball for on-the-move fielding and a
bent-arm, shoulder-height throw to hasten the
return.

Covering the Favoured Stroke

● *The Tactic*

If the captain has done his homework, covering a batsman's favourite stroke can pay early dividends and, even when faced with a new opponent, the more astute cricketer can identify his opponent's preferred way of batting within the first few balls he plays.

It is important for captains and bowlers to liaise on the tactics they feel will combat a player's favoured shots and may well choose to take the wicket-keeper's views into account.

By covering the shot a batsman is playing most confidently, a captain is supporting his bowler who may not always be able to prevent the shot by his own actions.

● *Learning the Tactic*

① There is a difference between a shot which will be chosen to hit a bad ball and a favoured stroke which is selected in defence or attack of good bowling. It is wrong of a skipper to change his field to cover the former and it is up to the bowler to correct his errors.

② If the preferred shot is the drive or cut it may have to be covered by boundary fielders as well as others in close positions.

③ It may be desirable to reduce the gap into which a favoured shot can be played rather than block it completely. The batsman will continue to feel it is vacant and take longer to realise he is not scoring so freely.

● *The Tactic in Use*

① A captain should aim to make the required changes quietly and thus gain another over or two before the batsman realises the shot is not scoring runs.

② In applying the tactic as described in 3 above, fielders can 'walk in' laterally as the ball is bowled, rather than straight towards the batsman, and so close gaps he saw before he settled into his stance.

● *Covering the Favoured Stroke: Andrew Hilditch, New Zealand v. Australia, Brisbane, 1985*

Although it was perhaps more of a weakness than a favoured stroke, Andrew Hilditch was always likely to attempt the hook at the short, straight ball and New Zealand ruthlessly use their knowledge of this in both innings of this match.

New Zealand win the toss and put Australia in. They meet with immediate reward as Hilditch hooks the fifth ball of the innings to Ewan Chatfield at long leg where he takes a well-judged catch above his head.

This incident only confirms what had been seen against England previously, that Hilditch seems incapable of stopping himself playing the hook when presented with the opportunity. Hence, in the second innings, the trap is set again with the long leg fieldsman in the identical position. Hilditch obliges and is once again caught there; his favoured shot has been covered, though in this instance he has been positively encouraged to keep playing it.

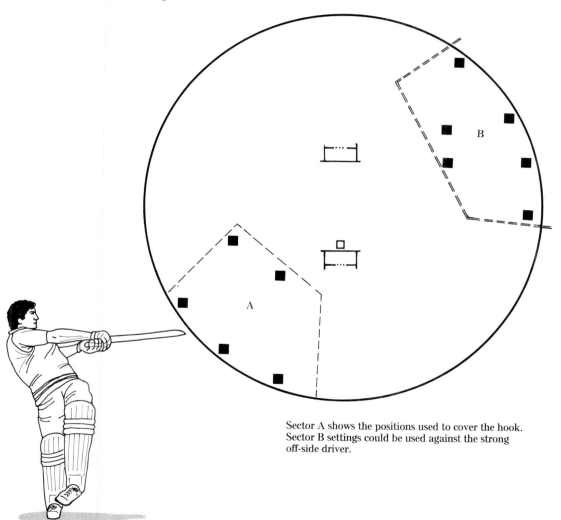

Sector A shows the positions used to cover the hook. Sector B settings could be used against the strong off-side driver.

Run-Outs

● *The Tactic*

There are few sights which excite spectators more than run-outs, and there is nothing more likely to exasperate a batsman than to get out in this manner. Run-outs can tilt the balance of a game, but can they be planned for, can they be considered a tactic to be deployed?

The answer is most certainly yes, because there have been teams which have achieved success on the back of a higher-than-average number of dismissals of this kind. These teams have trained to ensure that their fielders are alert to every chance of a run-out, keep their composure in such situations and know their personal roles and responsibilities.

With many club teams playing cricket which requires a result and, therefore, more often than not ends in a run chase, the prospect of run-outs is always increasing.

● *Learning the Tactic*

① Many run-outs follow a dabbed shot played short of the inner fielders, where the batsmen gamble on their running being quicker than the fielding side's pick-up and throw. Thus, cover-point, short mid-wicket and square leg are the positions where the quick run-in, pick-up and throw are often required.

② There are plenty of routines which can be practised by two or three fielders to hone

their skills in these positions. This is just one of those.

③ The bowler can increase the fielding side's chances in run-out situations if he is alive to covering the short-range shot and the need to regain a position by his stumps to complete a run-out.

● *The Tactic in Use*

① The whole team must watch for run-out opportunities, for the fielder on the opposite side of the field may be called upon to field a misdirected throw.

② Fielders at mid-on and mid-off must look to cover the bowler's stumps, particularly for the faster bowlers who have a longer follow-through.

● *Run-Outs: Allan Lamb, Northamptonshire v. Derbyshire, NatWest Trophy, Lord's, 1981*

Derbyshire win this tied match by virtue of losing fewer wickets, but observers put much of their victory down to three crucial run-outs.

Northants are put in but are not pressured unduly by the Derbyshire attack. It is the astute field placing of Derbyshire skipper Barry Wood and the superb fielding of his

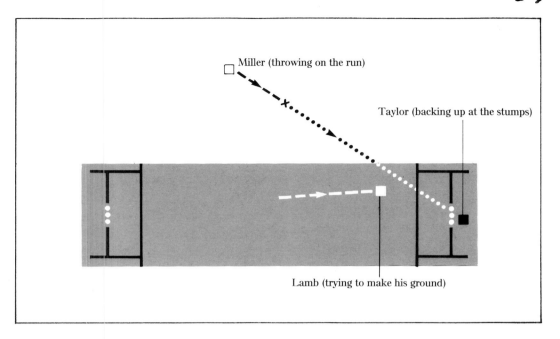

Miller (throwing on the run)

Taylor (backing up at the stumps)

Lamb (trying to make his ground)

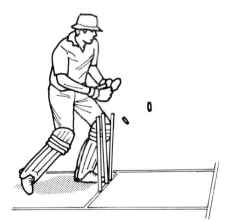

team which give them the edge. Yardley, Willey and Lamb are all run-out. The last was poised to make a large score when dismissed by a direct throw by Geoff Miller, collecting the ball on the run and throwing accurately in one swift movement.

Fitness

● *The Tactic*

Most players of sport will claim a certain level of fitness but few appreciate how their game could improve with a higher level of physical strength and agility. Such ideas have come later to cricket than to many other sports but the modern game demands that no eleven 'carries' unfit players.

At Test level the West Indies have set new standards and others are now following in their footsteps with individual training programmes and fitness routines.

Stamina is required by batsmen and bowlers alike, agility and suppleness by close fielders, sprinting speed by batsmen and fielders; thus, most fitness exercises are relevant to the game.

● *Learning the Tactic*

① Your fitness routines should be directed at your own cricketing needs. Leg and back strength for wicket-keepers, leg, arm and back power for fast bowlers, etc.

② Simple warming-up routines are advisable. The colder the day, the greater the need.

③ Fitness testing aids the understanding of personal needs. These tests can include body measurements, aerobic testing, muscular assessment and tests of speed, strength and flexibility.

● *The Tactic in Use*

① Superior fitness is demonstrable; opponents will soon notice if your fitness is greater than theirs.

② There is nothing wrong in exercising between deliveries when fielding or before batting. Sudden movements when cold or stiff can cause serious injury.

③ Mental fitness has its part to play. There are various books and magazines available which will assist the player who wants to enhance his confidence and concentration.

● *Fitness: Some Examples*

Of the many different exercises which can improve fitness for cricket, we show three which will strengthen wrists, arms, shoulders, chest and leg muscles and so benefit all players. Specialist players such as wicket-keepers, cover fieldsmen and fast bowlers will need to work on regimes which cater for their special needs.

① Standing erect with hands at your side and feet apart, grasp medium weight dumbbells in each hand and lower one weight whilst raising the other. Do not use heavy weights until you have done the routine regularly.

② With feet slightly apart and the weights held at your side, lift both dumbbells

upwards and outwards in a gentle movement and briefly hold that position before lowering the weights to their original position. During the exercise raise your heels, standing on the balls of your feet.

❸ Place one foot in front of the other and move into a partial crouch. Lift the back leg and the opposite arm as you raise your whole body onto the toes of the standing leg. Hold this position for a moment as you move your raised arm in front of your chest and the other behind your back.

Index